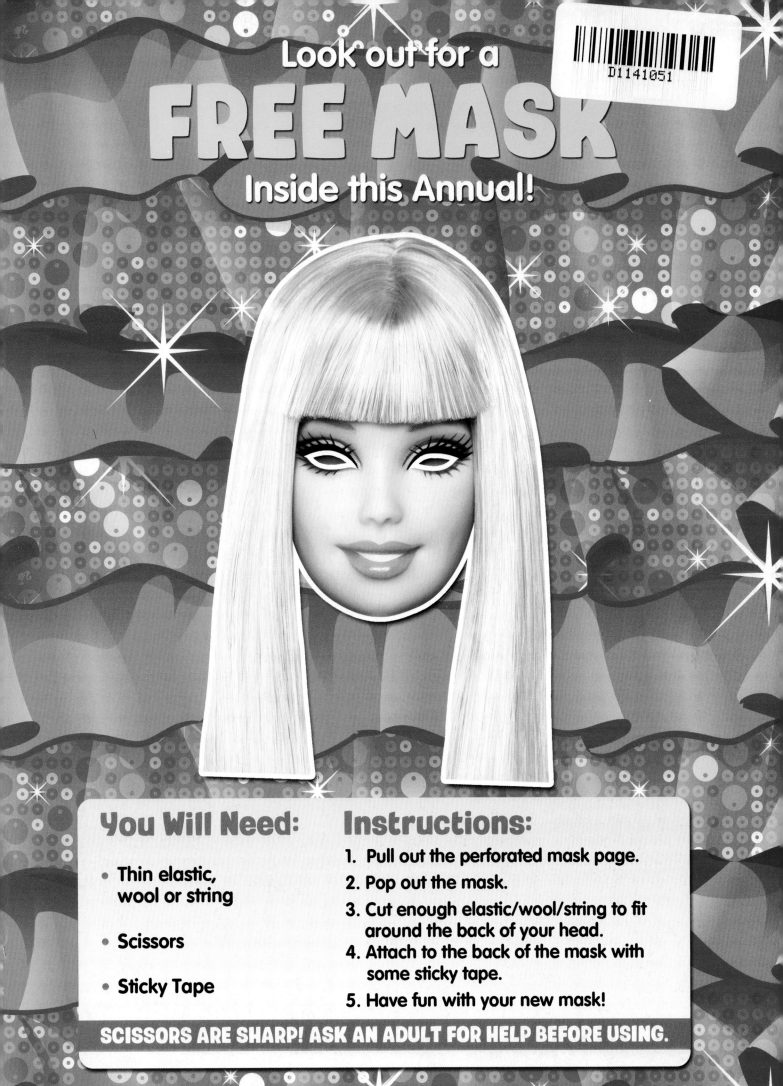

Look out for a
FREE MASK
Inside this Annual!

D1141051

You Will Need:

- Thin elastic, wool or string
- Scissors
- Sticky Tape

Instructions:

1. Pull out the perforated mask page.
2. Pop out the mask.
3. Cut enough elastic/wool/string to fit around the back of your head.
4. Attach to the back of the mask with some sticky tape.
5. Have fun with your new mask!

SCISSORS ARE SHARP! ASK AN ADULT FOR HELP BEFORE USING.

Contents

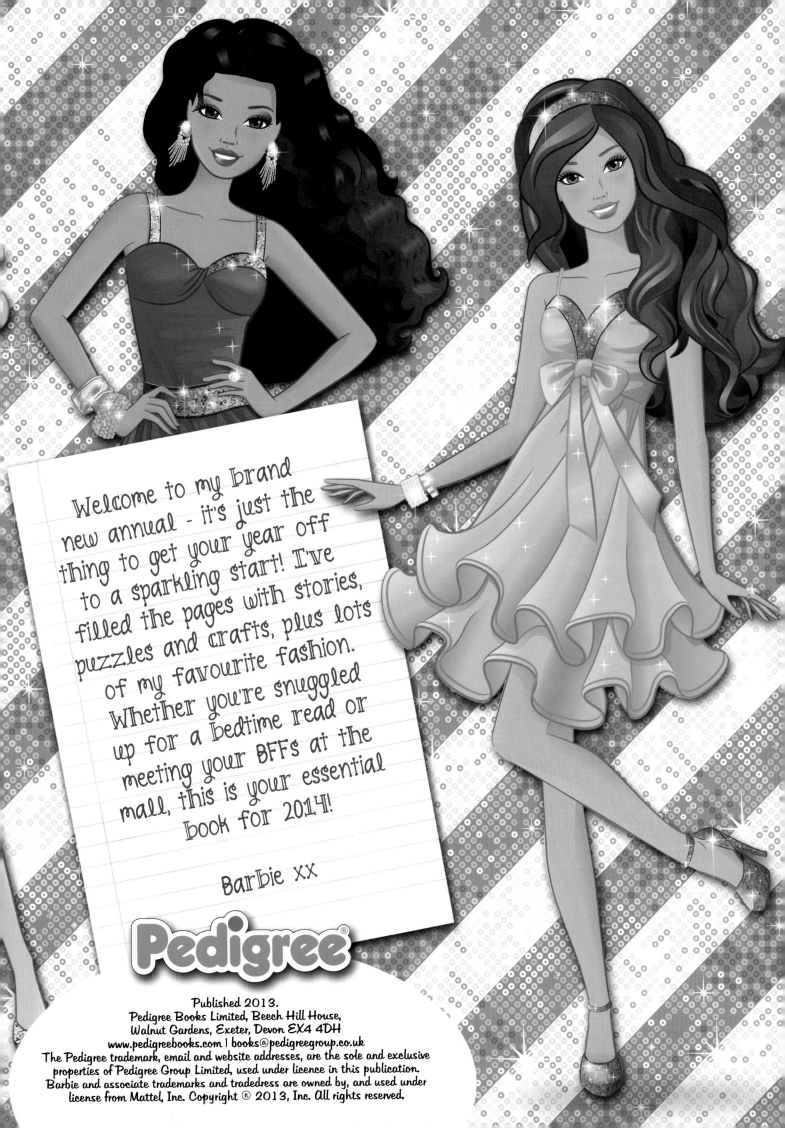

Welcome to my brand
new annual - it's just the
thing to get your year off
to a sparkling start! I've
filled the pages with stories,
puzzles and crafts, plus lots
of my favourite fashion.
Whether you're snuggled
up for a bedtime read or
meeting your BFFs at the
mall, this is your essential
book for 2014!

Barbie xx

Pedigree®

Published 2013.
Pedigree Books Limited, Beech Hill House,
Walnut Gardens, Exeter, Devon EX4 4DH
www.pedigreebooks.com | books@pedigreegroup.co.uk

Let it Sparkle!

When the first snowflake of winter falls, my heart flutters with excitement! I love walking in the park, meeting my friends for hot chocolate and Christmas shopping for my little sisters! It's a time for wrapping up in winter woollies by day, then glitzing up in festive sparkles when the evening comes.

This my new party dress. Do you like it? The skirt is embellished with tiny silver sequins.

Barbie's winter style

★ Diamanté luxe silver shoes
★ Cosy winter knits
★ Colour pop accessories

Festive favourites

★ Snowball fights with Steven and Ken
★ Sleepovers with my girls
★ A new pair of winter boots
★ Walking Sequin in the park

The Essential Barbie

Eyes:
Blue

Hair:
Golden blonde

Height:
170cm

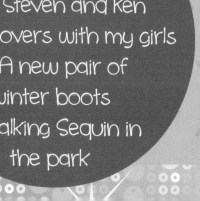

6

This page is reserved exclusively for you! Draw a portrait of yourself in your favourite outfit, then write down the little things that make you special. What will you be doing and what will you be wearing this winter? I can't wait to find out!

The Essential Me

Eyes:
....

Hair:
....

Height:
....

Favourite colour:
....

Draw your picture here. When you've finished, colour it in using your brightest pencils or crayons.

My winter style

....
....
....

Festive favourites

....
....
....
....

Now that we've said hi, would you like to meet my sisters, too? Skipper, Stacie and Chelsea are all waiting on page 12...

Mixed Up Mall

I've just had a terrific trip to the mall with Nikki - that girl loves, loves, LOVES to shop! Want to know what we bought today? All you have to do is rearrange the letters and write them in the spaces below. The shapes will help you guess.

1 SRDES

_ _ _ _ _

2 IALN LPHISO

_ _ _ _ _ _ _ _ _

3 NDHAAGB

_ _ _ _ _ _ _

4 SPILGSOL

_ _ _ _ _ _ _ _

5 SOBOT

_ _ _ _ _

You can find all the answers on page 77!

Sketch and Skate

I have a brand new winter hobby. I'm learning to ice dance! It's so wonderful whirling and twirling around the rink to the sound of music.
Would you like a to draw a portrait of me in my sparkly skating costume?
All you have to do is copy each square from the top picture into the matching one in the empty grid underneath. When you're finished, colour your artwork in.

My first solo ballet performance. My heart fluttered all the way through!

Picture This!

When it's too cold to go out I like to snuggle up and work on my scrapbook. Do you have one? It's a special place for sticking in pictures and writing about special memories.

Help me caption these photos. I've done the first one to get you started. Find a pen and imagine what might be happening in each shot.

Shh... Surprise!

Christmas is the season to sparkle! This year I've found some really special gifts for my family and friends. I can't wait to see their faces when they unwrap them!

Every present is a secret. I don't want to spoil the surprise. If you can crack the code, you can sneak a peek! Use the Key to help you work out which letter each number represents.

Chelsea
20 5 4 4 25 2 5 1 18
‾ ‾ ‾ ‾ ‾ ‾ ‾ ‾ ‾

Raquelle
13 9 18 18 15 18
‾ ‾ ‾ ‾ ‾ ‾

Ryan
2 15 15 11
‾ ‾ ‾ ‾

Skipper
8 5 1 4 16 8 15 14 5 19
‾ ‾ ‾ ‾ ‾ ‾ ‾ ‾ ‾ ‾

Stacie
20 18 1 9 14 5 18 19
‾ ‾ ‾ ‾ ‾ ‾ ‾ ‾

Teresa
7 12 15 22 5 19
‾ ‾ ‾ ‾ ‾ ‾

Key:

A	B	C	D	E	F	G	H	I	J	K	L	M	N	O	P	Q	R	S	T	U	V	W	X	Y	Z
1	2	3	4	5	6	7	8	9	10	11	12	13	14	15	16	17	18	19	20	21	22	23	24	25	26

WINTER DELIGHTS

It's brilliant being big sister to Skipper, Stacie and Chelsea. It's like having three ready-made best friends! The girls come over to my place all the time. Although each one of us is very different, together we make a great combination. We love sledging, sleepovers and watching Christmassy movies.

Eyes:
Lavender

Hair:
Brunette with a purple streak

Height:
155cm

Pets:
Scrunchie

The essential Skipper

Skipper is super-connected! She's a loyal sister, who always makes time to text me or email a funny picture message. Skipper records a brilliant video blog that has followers all over the world.

SKIPPER'S STYLE IS QUIRKY AND CREATIVE, JUST LIKE HER!

The essential Stacie

When I need to blow the cobwebs away, I call Stacie! My middle sister is a sporty girl who's always up for a game of netball or a run round the park. Stacie is enthusiastic, kind and great fun to be with!

STACIE ISN'T A GIRLIE GIRL, BUT SHE ALWAYS LOOKS STYLISH AND FRESH!

The essential
Chelsea

Chelsea is my adorable baby sister. She may have a lot of growing up to do, but she's already proved herself to be a natural star! When Chelsea steps in front of the camera, she always steals the show.

CHELSEA IS MY ADORABLE BABY SISTER - DRESSING UP IS HER FAVOURITE THING.

Eyes:
Blue

Hair:
Blonde and long

Height:
107cm

Pets:
Slipper

Eyes:
Twinkly blue

Hair:
Honey blonde

Height:
137cm

Pets:
Rugby

I heart those three so much! Now it's time to introduce to my friends. Flip to page 34 to meet Teresa, Nikki, Raquelle and Summer!

13

Lost for Words

Dear

Thought you'd like a 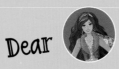 from my latest movie set! I'm shooting the film in . The other is my very good friend . The weather is very chilly and are starting to fall. Luckily we get to wrap up in s and . We miss you guys! Please send our ♥ to , and .

Barbie xxx

No matter where I go in the world, I always make time to keep in touch with my girlfriends. Today I wrote a card to my favourite BBF! Look at each pictures clue, then choose the best word to fill in the blanks.

Movie Magic

Last night I was nominated with a statue for my latest movie – it was a complete surprise! Ken was the perfect date for the awards ceremony. We had so much fun dressing up and having our photos taken.
Join up the dots to show Ken and I on the red carpet.

Colour in the picture to finish it!

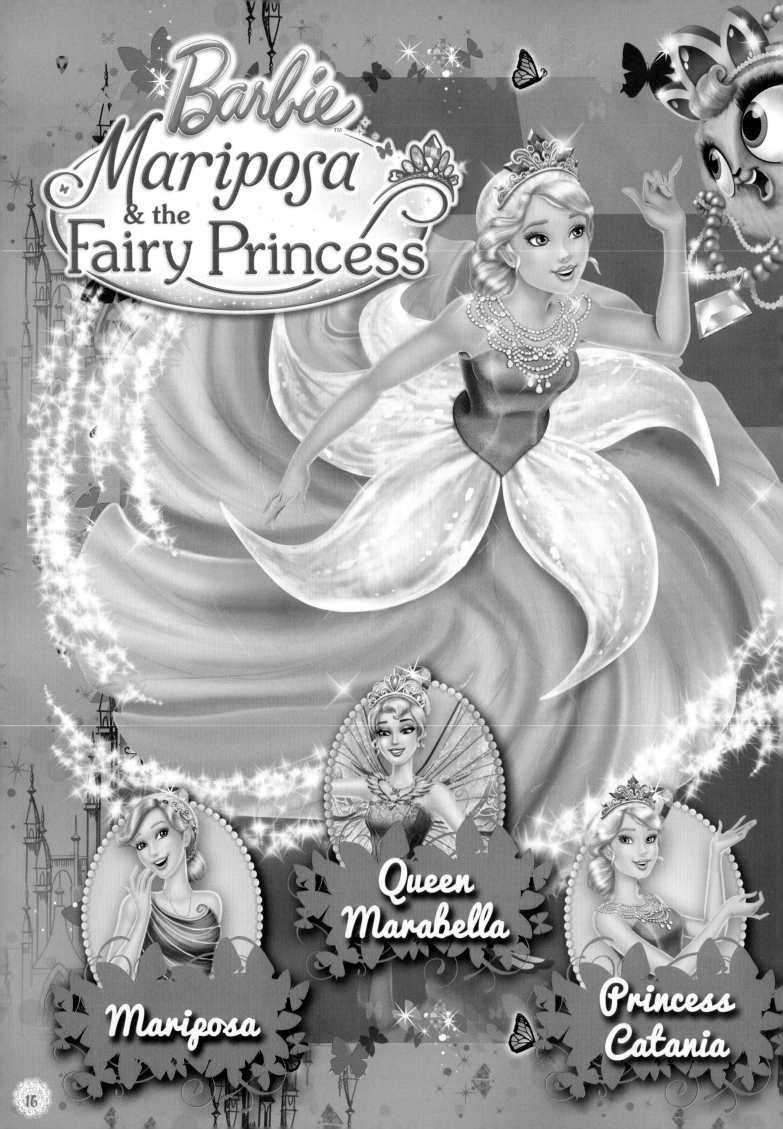

Barbie
Mariposa
& the
Fairy Princess

Mariposa

Queen
Marabella

Princess
Catania

It was another enchanting morning in Flutterfield. Mariposa smiled as she flew through the magical land with her good friend, Willa. Fairy after fairy greeted or waved to them happily. Everybody was thrilled to see Mariposa today! Suddenly, a furry pink fluffball darted into view – Zee! She'd come to tell Mariposa that the Queen wanted to see her right away.
"Lead the way," said Mariposa.
They rushed towards the royal palace.

'The best way make a friend is to be a frien

Talayla

King Regellius

18

It was another enchanting morning in Flutterfield. Mariposa smiled as she flew through the magical land with her good friend, Willa. Fairy after fairy greeted or waved to them happily. Everybody was thrilled to see Mariposa today! Suddenly, a furry pink fluffball darted into view – Zee! She'd come to tell Mariposa that the Queen wanted to see her right away.

"Lead the way," said Mariposa.

They rushed towards the royal palace.

'The best way to
make a friend
is to be a friend.'

Talayla

King
Regellius

Queen Marabella, Prince Carlos and Lord Gastrous were waiting in the throne room. They asked Mariposa what she knew about the Crystal Fairies of Shimmervale.

"Their land is built on an amazing natural energy source called Crystallites," began Mariposa. "We Butterfly Fairies and the Crystal Fairies were friends, until the King of Shimmervale accused us of stealing the Crystallites."

"Mariposa, go to Shimmervale as Flutterfield's royal ambassador," Queen Marabella decided. "Prove that Butterfly Fairies and Crystal Fairies can be friends."

Mariposa wasn't sure she wanted to go so far from Flutterfield, but Prince Carlos gave her a beautiful Flutter Flower to remind her of home.

Visitors to Shimmervale always received a grand welcome, but when Mariposa arrived no one came out to greet her. A lone Crystal Fairy called Talayla showed the guest to her palace bedchamber.

"It's covered in thorns!" gasped Mariposa.

Talayla nodded proudly. "I based it on everything we Crystal Fairies know about the Butterfly Fairies!"

Talayla took Mariposa to meet King Regellius and his daughter Princess Catania. The Princess was accompanied by her friends Anu and Sylvie the Pegasus.

"I love how your Crystallites shimmer in the sun," smiled Mariposa, reaching up to touch a chandelier.

"Get away!" bellowed the King. "The Crystallites can only be touched by the Crystal Fairies."

Mariposa was very sorry, but then her large Butterfly Fairy wings began to unfurl.

"Those wings are a menace!" declared the King. "Keep them out of the way!"

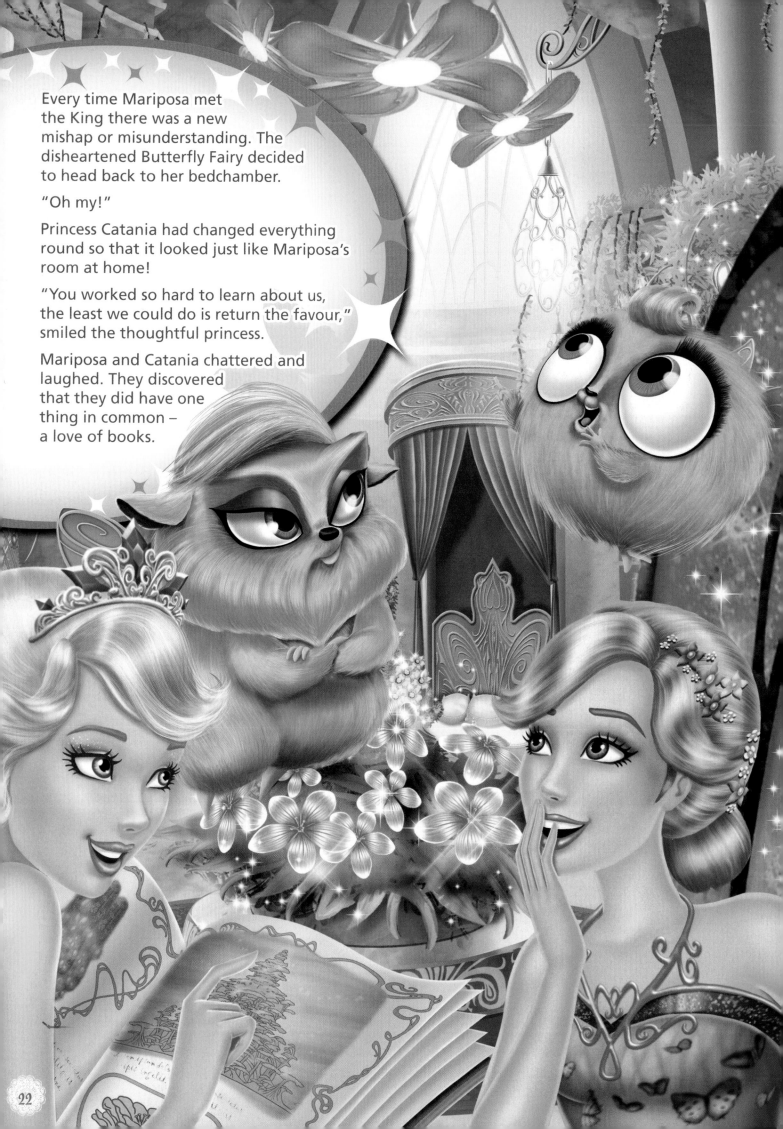

Every time Mariposa met the King there was a new mishap or misunderstanding. The disheartened Butterfly Fairy decided to head back to her bedchamber.

"Oh my!"

Princess Catania had changed everything round so that it looked just like Mariposa's room at home!

"You worked so hard to learn about us, the least we could do is return the favour," smiled the thoughtful princess.

Mariposa and Catania chattered and laughed. They discovered that they did have one thing in common – a love of books.

Princess Catania took Mariposa to her favourite reading spot – a chamber perched high atop Shimmervale Palace. The Heartstone was kept here, the most precious Crystallite in the whole kingdom. Afterwards they went to Glow Waterfalls.

"It's good to be back after so long," sighed Catania.

The Princess told a story from many years' ago. One day a bitter old fairy called the Gwyllion froze Catania's wings because the King wouldn't give her a Crystallite. Poor Catania had fallen from the sky. She had never flown on her own again.

Princess Catania held out a glittering Crystallite necklace.

"I want you to have this," she said.

"I c-c-can't," stuttered Mariposa. "No Butterfly Fairy should ever take a Crystallite from Shimmervale."

"You're not taking it," insisted Catania, "it's a gift."

Mariposa also had a present to give – the Flutter Flower.

"After I leave, this can remind you of me!" she said.

The friends headed back to the palace. That evening the Crystal Ball was taking place. It was Mariposa's big chance to win over the Fairies of Shimmervale!

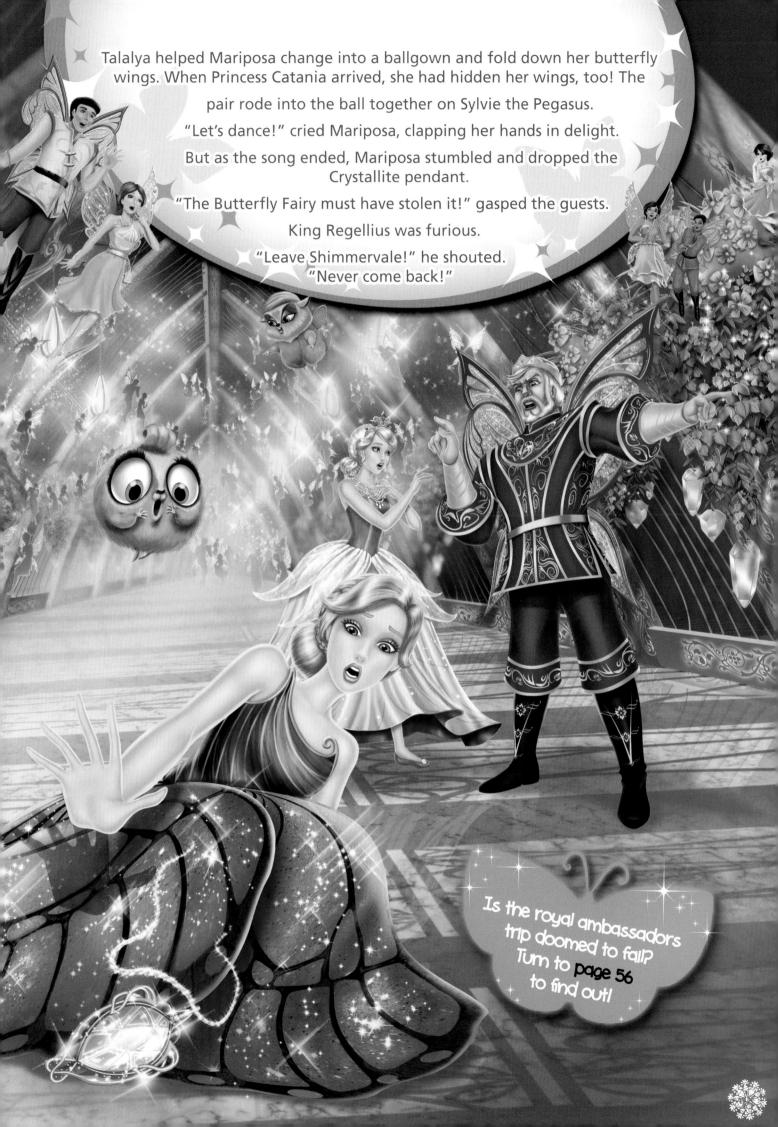

Talalya helped Mariposa change into a ballgown and fold down her butterfly wings. When Princess Catania arrived, she had hidden her wings, too! The pair rode into the ball together on Sylvie the Pegasus.

"Let's dance!" cried Mariposa, clapping her hands in delight.

But as the song ended, Mariposa stumbled and dropped the Crystallite pendant.

"The Butterfly Fairy must have stolen it!" gasped the guests.

King Regellius was furious.

"Leave Shimmervale!" he shouted. "Never come back!"

Is the royal ambassadors trip doomed to fail? Turn to page 56 to find out!

Shimmering

Despite their differences, Mariposa and Princess Catania quickly found that they shared lots of things in common. The fairies both adored reading, talking and dancing! On the night of the Crystal Ball, the friends put on beautiful ballgowns and twirled around the floor.

Sensations!

Use your prettiest crayons, pencils or felt-tips to bring the palace ballroom to life! Afterwards you could even stick on sequins and glitter, or decorate the fairies with shimmering gel pens.

Scholastic Fantastic

Do you enjoy school? Malibu High is a great place to learn! Whether it's a field trip or an art class - there's always something new to discover.

There are ten school related words hiding in this letter grid. Can you circle every one. The words can run in any direction. Search by running your finger forwards and backwards along the rows, then up and down the diagonals, too.

INK

DESK

TEST

PENCIL

RUCKSACK

COMPUTER

BOOK

RULER

HOMEWORK

CALCULATOR

H	O	M	E	W	O	R	K	R	L
B	Y	G	C	V	D	U	M	U	F
C	O	I	P	E	N	C	I	L	E
O	H	S	J	K	F	K	T	E	U
M	T	I	W	C	L	S	B	R	D
P	A	N	Q	M	E	A	Z	E	K
U	R	K	P	T	J	C	S	N	T
T	X	P	D	N	G	K	O	O	B
E	I	J	Q	H	R	S	A	X	E
R	O	T	A	L	U	C	L	A	C

Bags and Bling

Fashion is all about choices! Slipping on the right necklace, shoes and belt can transform a plain outfit into something truly sensational. Would you be my stylist today? Read through my schedule, then draw a line to match each activity up to the perfect accessory.

A workout at the gym.

Dancing at the Christmas Snow Ball.

A winter's stroll with Sequin.

A busy trip into city.

Becoming prom princess!

Perfectly Polished

I always try to look my best and that means taking care of myself inside and out! My beauty advice is simple. Every one of us is beautiful, we just need to know how to make ourselves shine. Here are my top ten tips on looking perfectly polished every day of the week.

1 *Rest!* The first tip is very simple. Be sure you get your sleep! Ten good hours every night will banish dark shadows and help you feel bright-eyed and raring to go.

2 *Sort!* It's hard to choose clothes from a cluttered closet! Your favourite things will get creased or hidden. Every three months, hang your clothes neatly and give to charity the items you really don't wear anymore.

3 *Plan!* If you've got a special date in the calendar, allow plenty of time to plan what you are going to wear from head to toe. This will avoid a panic on the day and you'll feel a million dollars before you step out the door.

4 *Gloss!* Nails look elegant if they're cared for properly. File them into neat rounded shapes, then moisturize the cuticles with a little oil. Gloss on some pale polish and your nails will look pretty and clean.

5 *Protect!* Your skin won't look its best if you don't give it a little care. Wear sunscreen on warm days. Even winter sun can cause damage. Use a brush to massage your skin in the shower, then slick on some body butter or cream.

6 *Pamper!* Invite your BFFs round for a pamper evening once a month. While you giggle and chat, give each other face packs or wrap your hair in a deep conditioning treatment. You'll look and smell gorgeous afterwards!

7 *Brush!* Give your tresses a model shine by brushing your hair for five minutes every morning and night. There are lots of great de-tangler brushes you can use if your locks are long or very curly.

8 *Make-up!* Cosmetics are fun, but you only need a little bit! Experiment at home until you learn the best way to put it on. A touch of blusher and a slick of pearly lipgloss are all you need to look party-perfect.

9 *Accessorise!* When you're all dressed up, take a moment to look in the mirror. A well-chosen hairclip or a brooch might be just the thing you need to set off your outfit.

10 *Smile!* Did you know that you can smile with both your mouth and your eyes? A genuine smile will make your true beauty shine.

Ready to Party!

I always smile when I see this shot! It shows me and my friends all dressed up for a party at Steven's house. It took hours to curl Nikki's hair and even longer to help Raquelle pick which earrings to wear! It was all worth it. The party was a sparkling success.

Can you spot five differences between the two photos? Use a pencil or crayon to circle the things that have been changed

It's a Barbie World!

We know each other so well now, I think you're ready to play my picture quiz! All you have to do is read through each question and tick the picture that answers it. Can you score ten out of ten? Find a pencil and give it a try!

1 Who did I find lost in the park?

Blissa

Sequin

Taffy

2 What's the name of my littlest sister?

Chelsea

Skipper

Stacie

3 What did my friends surprise me with on my last birthday?

Lacey

Shoes

Handbag

4 Which of the boys always makes me laugh?

Ken

Ryan

Steven

5 What's my new winter hobby?

 Ice Skating ○

 Tennis ○

 Dolphin training ○

6 Which of my friends is a famous catwalk model?

 Summer ○

 Raquelle ○

 Teresa ○

7 What's my favourite colour?

Red ○

Blue ○

Pink ○

8 Which of these adorable creatures is called Slipper?

 A ○

 B ○

 C ○

9 Which of my sisters is totally into technology?

 Skipper ○

 Stacie ○

 Chelsea ○

10 Where are you most likely to find me on the weekend?

Home ○

School ○

Racetrack ○

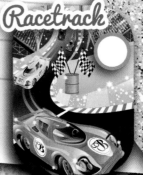

Finished? Well done! Colour in a pretty snowflake.

Don't forget to check your answers on page 77.

Glitter Girls

My girls are there for me winter, spring, summer and fall! Teresa, Nikki, Raquelle and Summer share my secrets, make me giggle and give me honest advice whenever I need it. Whether I'm working the runway in Paris or filming a movie in London, I know the fab four are just a phone call away! We're shopping buddies, school mates and BFFs.

The Essential Nikki

Nikki says it like it is and I love her for that! I know I can trust her to tell me the truth – Nikki sticks by her friends through thick and thin. She's an amazing actress and a graceful dancer.

Nikki is the ultimate fashionista, she is more into vintage clothes! This ruched cocktail dress is so on-trend.

The Essential Teresa

Teresa has been my best friend since we met in ballet class when we were four years old! She's kind-hearted, sweet and always sees the good in everyone. Teresa has a major soft spot for animals.

Teresa is arty with an amazing eye for colour. Look how cleverly she layers pink, orange and sky blue!

Eyes:
Hazel

Hair:
Brown with reddish-brown highlights, long and wavy

Height:
173cm

Pets:
Tika and Tiki

Eyes:
Brown

Hair:
Dark brown with golden highlights

Height:
173cm

Pets:
Sutton

The Essential Raquelle

Raquelle can be hard to get to know, but deep down there's a sweet girl trying to get out! She is a sought after catwalk model who can carry off all the latest designer looks. Her twin brother Ryan is also in the gang.

No wonder the camera loves Raquelle! This glamorous jewelled dress is the ultimate style statement.

Eyes:
Blue

Hair:
Black

Height:
178cm

Pets:
None

The Essential Summer

Summer is full of beans, 24/7! She often pops round at the weekend to challenge me to a game of tennis or a workout at the gym. No matter what's going on at home or at school, I can count on Summer to make me smile.

Summer's look is natural and sooo pretty. Her loose twisted plait tops off her outfit perfectly.

Eyes:
Green

Hair:
Light reddish brown

Height:
170cm

Pets:
None

So now you've got to see the girls, we should bring on the guys! Ken, Steven and Ryan are waiting to meet you on page 68.

Let's go in the SNOW!

If the weather outside is frightful, go and do something delightful! There's no need to hide away on wintry days. Layer up in hats and scarves, pull on your boots, then explore your local park or garden. Whether you're a sporty girl or an arty type, everyone can have fun in the great outdoors.

BUILD A DEN

Invite some friends to dress-up in old clothes and start den building. Gather fallen branches and twigs, then build a lean-to or domed teepee. How will you keep your den warm and dry? Try covering the structure with different materials such as leaves or things that you can find on the ground.

BE ALLERGY AWARE. CHECK WITH AN ADULT THAT IT'S OK BEFORE TOUCHING PEANUT BUTTER.

MAKE A BIRD FEEDER

Winter is tough for birds that don't fly away to warm climates. You can help the birds in your garden by making a bird feeder? Tie a long piece of string to an old pine cone. Using a spoon smear peanut butter all over the cone, pressing it into the gaps. Next, roll the sticky cone in birdseed until it's covered all over. Tie a loop in the top of the string and hang your birdfeeder out for the local wildlife to enjoy!

ENJOY NATURE

Mounting your own wildlife watch really is very easy your most important pieces of Kit are your eyes! Find a notebook, magnifying glass and pencils then explore. Look for animal footprints, listen for birdcalls, and sketch flowers and plants. Use your notes to make a unique nature book of your area. You could stick in some leaves and twigs that you discover.

BARBIE'S COLD WEATHER RULES

♥ WRAP UP IN SNUGGLY CLOTHES
♥ KEEP MOVING
♥ DON'T CATCH A CHILL
♥ WARM UP WITH A HOT CHOCOLATE

SCAVENGER HUNT

Make a list of 20 items that you might find outside near you. You could start with a rock, a leaf, a seed or a twig shaped in a 'V'? Copy your list and share it out with your friends making sure they each have a basket. Set a time limit of one hour for a hunt. Who will find the most objects from your list?

ICE SCULPTURES

This arty project takes 24 hours and is worth the wait! Fill some balloons with water and a few different drops of food colouring to each. Ask a grown-up to help you tie a Knot in the balloons. Leave them outside overnight to freeze. When you get up, peel away the balloons. Enjoy the brightly-coloured balls sparkling in the frosty morning air!

HOST WINTER GAMES

Use glitter pens and card to make some cute medals, then invite your friends outside to compete in a special winter sports day. Run races, ride bikes, play winter rounders and enter mock ski slaloms the possibilities are endless! When you're all puffed out, hold a medal ceremony to congratulate the winners.

AND IF IT SNOWS, WHY NOT...

- BUILD A SNOW PRINCESS
- GO SLEDGING
- MAKE SNOW ANGELS
- THROW SNOWBALLS
- SKETCH SNOW FLAKES

"Cupcakes?" squeal Stacie and Chelsea.

Barbie scoops up her mixing bowl. These treats are for Teresa!

"She always says that I'm a klutz in the kitchen," sighs Barbie, "so I bet her a pedicure that I could do this!"

They've got to be perfect!

Can we help?

Stacie and Chelsea both want in!

Barbie raises an eyebrow. "Er... hello? You girls aren't exactly great cooks either," she reminds them. "Remember spaghetti night?"

"We won't mess up this time. Promise!"

"How's Malibu's most fabulous girl?" asks Ken.

"Frazzled!" replies Barbie. "I'll be trimming Teresa's tootsies if I don't come up with some cupcakes pronto."

Ken doesn't hang around. If Barbie needs help, he is all over it!

Hey doll!

Before Barbie can say 'cupcake crisis', Ken dashes down to the basement and gets to work.

"Isn't he the best boyfriend ever?" she coos.

Totally chivalrous!

Don't worry Barbie!

Ta-daa!

"A toaster?" exclaims Barbie.

"It only looks like a toaster," chuckles Ken. "It's actually a

fully automated cupcake maker!"

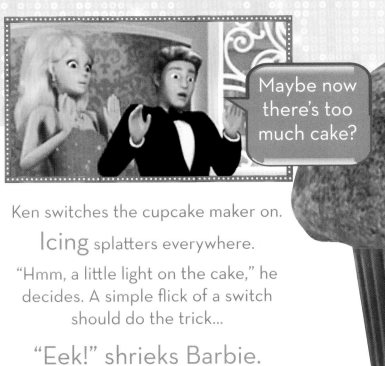

Maybe now there's too much cake?

Ken switches the cupcake maker on.

Icing splatters everywhere.

"Hmm, a little light on the cake," he decides. A simple flick of a switch should do the trick...

"Eek!" shrieks Barbie.

Barbie is right on course for another **pedi penalty!**

"I really don't want to lose this bet," she shudders. "Last time was bad enough."

One way or another, she has to make the **scrummiest** cupcakes ever!

Ugggh!

I have the perfect thing for this.

"It's behind all the gifts you get and never use. I wouldn't want to be the guy that bought those **lame gifts**," groans Ken.

Awkward!

"Aha!" cries Barbie, finding it.

"The Little Miss Cupcakelator."

"Teresa just called!" yells Stacie. "She's on her way.

We need cupcakes **fast!**"

Easy peasy! Barbie switches on the Little Miss Cupcakelator.

"Wow!"

Three perfect cupcake towers made in a trice!

Ok! That's enough.

Barbie's gadget just keeps on
cooking up cupcakes...

"I said, 'that's enough'."

"Where's the off switch?" shouts Ken.

Uh-oh! Barbie remembers what happened
the last time she used the
Little Miss Cupcakelator...

There is no off switch!

Teresa will be here any minute.

"The place looks like a
bakery has **pooped**
its pants," sighs Ken.

Time is running out! There's
only one thing to do.

"**Stash them!**"
squeaks Barbie.

Everyone stuffs the
cupcakes into cupboards.

"Hi Teresa," smiles Barbie.
"I whipped up some
cupcakes for you."

"No way! You made these?"

CR-ASH! Barbie's cupcake
stash tumbles all over the kitchen.

Teresa grins. It's
pedi payback time!

Ready when you are!

The End

HAPPY BIRTHDAY, CHELSEA!

Chelsea was so **excited**, she woke up before the first toot of her alarm. The morning she'd been **waiting** for had finally arrived! It was **Chelsea's birthday** - her favourite day of the year. She was so happy.

Yipee! It's the best day ever!

Happy birthday, Chelsea!

Skipper stuck her head round the door telling Chelsea her **breakfast** was ready. Stacie and Barbie were busy making sure that Chelsea's **sixth** birthday was the **best** ever!

Perfect birthdays don't happen by themselves.

Stacie took birthdays very seriously. **So**, while she gave orders to Barbie and Skipper, Ken was in the **garage** putting Chelsea's gift together. It was a **cute new bike!**

Piece of cake!

Ken couldn't wait to surprise Chelsea.... .... and **impress** Barbie with his technical expertise!

Barbie and Stacie made a **special birthday breakfast** for the special birthday girl.

"Awesome!" shrieked Chelsea.

Skipper had to **decorate** quickly. She sighed. "Ken **never complains** when he's got jobs to do," Barbie reminded her.

Ken was at least trying **very hard** not to moan. "I can't believe how one kids bike could arrive in **so many pieces!**" Ken gasped.

Skipper carried a box into the living room. The way she saw it, she'd **definitely** been given the **hardest job.**

Meanwhile, making Chelsea's **birthday cake** took Stacie at least five minutes.

Skipper reached over and pressed a **button**.
As if by magic streamers, banners and balloons dropped down from the ceiling.

Job done!

That wasn't so bad.

Er... I've no idea!

Barbie took her baby sister upstairs to play.
"Guess what I **really** want for my birthday," teased Chelsea.
"A carousel?" asked Barbie.
Chelsea shook her head.
Barbie **couldn't** guess right!

How's it going, Ken?

I'm winning!

It was time to give Chelsea her **presents**. Skipper went to check on Ken but the bike didn't look much like a bike. He wouldn't show Skipper the **tennis-playing-wheelie-thingy** with a life of it's own.

Chelsea thanked her sisters for another brilliant birthday. "I'm having the best time ever!" she smiled.

There was just one teeny tiny thing missing.

Ken appeared at just the right moment. He'd finally managed to construct Chelsea's bike!

Chelsea still wanted one thing none of the gang could have guessed ever! A tennis-playing-wheelie-thingy. Ken fainted. There's no pleasing some dolls!

The End

Livin' the Dream

I'm all dressed up and ready for a lovely evening out with my girlfriends - Teresa's picking me up in five! Where do you think we might be heading? The answer is hidden in this fab riddle. Read the lines, write down the letters and the mystery will be solved!

My first begins mall and merry-go-round,
My second's in lost, but also in found,
My third is in velvet, it's written there twice,
My fourth is in indigo and of course ice,
My fifth is in earring and emerald too,
My sixth starts the secret I'm sharing with you.

I'm going to the...

_ _ _ _ _ _ !

Sequin Search

Today I popped to the vets with Sequin - it's time for her annual pet check. She was a little nervous at first, for a big hug soon changed that!

A

B

C

D

Take a look at these photos at the vets surgery. One snap is slightly different to the rest. Can you spot the odd-one-out? Colour in the bone beside it.

Make Everyday Fabulous!

Daywear

Decisions, decisions - when it comes to fashion, I'm spoilt for choice! Will you be my stylist? Take a look through my closet, then pick your favourite looks for day and night. Use pencils or felt-tip pens to colour each outfit in. With your eye for design, I'm sure to look fabulous!

Cute hearts and denim

Fun and fashionable!

Laidback layers

Sporty cropped joggers

Eveningwear

Totally
frou frou

Baby-doll
Barbie

Stepping out
in sparkles

Stepping out
in sparkles

Try using
stickers or
glitter pens
to give your
colouring
some extra
sparkle!

Makeover Maze

Uh-oh, I've only got half an hour to get out of the tub and make my way into town! Will you help me work some makeover magic? Draw a line through the maze, showing me the quickest route to meet my friends. Please hurry, I can't be late for the gang!

Start

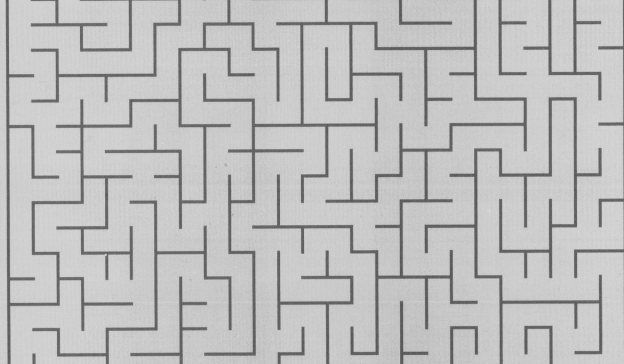

Finish!

Happy Hair

Make your own headband holder!

I love styling my hair, but it can be hard keeping track of all those headbands, clips and scrunchies. My dressing table is covered with them! Luckily I've found a solution. This homemade headband holder doesn't just look pretty, it does a brilliant job, too. Why don't you give it a try?

You will need:

♥ A round empty canister, such as a baby formula container

♥ A few pieces of pretty giftwrap paper

♥ Ruler ♥ Pencil

♥ Rounded scissors ♥ PVA glue

Always ask a grown-up to help when using scissors.

1 Use a ruler to measure strips of giftwrap paper that are 4cm wide and 4cm deeper than the height of your canister. Mark the strips with a pencil, then cut them out.

2 Keep going until you have 15 strips in at least two patterns of giftwrap.

3 Take one of the strips and coat it with glue. Turn the canister so that the lid is at the bottom. Now stick the strip onto the side of it. Add a contrasting strip of giftwrap next to the first, allowing it to overlap a little bit.

4 Stick strips all the way round the canister, until the whole tub is covered. When they are dry, fold the strips over the bottom of the canister and glue them in place.

5 Turn the canister over and fill it with scrunchies and clips, then put the lid on to keep them safe. Now slide headbands around the outside. Your headband holder is ready to go!

Get Connected

Skipper has a gadget for everything - she's a social media princess!
Sometimes however, you just need to operate the old-fashioned way.
Skipper is trying to text me, but I can't hear the phone. I'm too busy
dancing at the disco with my friends!

Can you help my little sister?
Which trail will lead Skipper to the disco?
Circle the correct letter.

a B c

You made it!

Make, Bake and Decorate!

This afternoon. Teresa is treating Chelsea and I to our own private baking lesson. She's amazing in the kitchen! A batch of gorgeous Christmas biscuits are on the menu today. Would you like to join us? The recipe will tell you just what to do.

Ovens are hot. Always ask an adult to help you before getting to work in the kitchen.

Make your own Christmas Cookies

Ingredients

♥ 1 egg

♥ 140g icing sugar

♥ 1 teaspoon vanilla extract

♥ 250g softened butter

♥ 375g plain flour.

plus extra for sprinkling

 Ask a grown-up to help you separate the egg from its white. Pour the yolk into a mixing bowl. then add in the icing sugar. vanilla extract and butter. Stir everything together with a spoon.

 Tip in the flour and mix the ingredients into a dough. Pick out the dough and shape it with your hands into a round tube.

 Cover the dough in plastic food wrap. then put it in the fridge for half an hour to firm up. Ask your helper to turn the oven on to 180°C/160°F/Gas Mark 4 and line a baking tray with greaseproof paper.

 Take the chilled dough out of the fridge and sprinkle some flour on the worktop. Roll out the dough until it is as thick as your finger. Use cookie cutters to press out biscuit shapes and a skewer to press a round hole at the top of each shape. Pop them on the baking sheet

 Put the biscuits in the oven for 15 mins or until golden brown. Get help putting them on a wire rack to cool.

Festive Decorating

Get creative! Ice your biscuits in Christmassy colours. Add writing. silver flakes or little edible stars. Thread ribbon through each one and hang it on your tree.

Christmas Crossword

What do the holidays mean to you? For me the season is all about thinking of others and celebrating with the people you love. This crossword is full of words to get you in a festive frame of mind. Read the clues then write the answers into the blank spaces.

ACROSS

1. The animals that pull Santa's sleigh.

2. Twinkly garlands used for decorating.

3. Another name for Father Christmas.

4. The winged ornament that sits on the top of a Christmas tree.

5. A good character who's a halo above their head.

DOWN

1. A round decoration that hangs from a ribbon.

2. A festive bush with bright red berries.

3. A holy Christmas song.

4. A pretty garland for the front door.

5. The colour of the Christmas tree.

6. A bright light in the night sky.

Divine Dresses

I'm such a lucky girl.
my wardrobe twinkles with rackfuls
of stunning evening gowns! Let me
model some for you. If I try each one
on. will you choose the outfit that
works the best?
Colour in a heart next to your
favourite look.

Beautiful pink sparkly cocktail dress
with a baby-pink bow.

French-style two-piece with
a glitzy pink belt.

Simple yet gorgeous
soft pink dress.

Contrast two-piece
with stunning gold-shimmer underskirt.

Gold and blue two-piece with
contrasting pink belt.

"I have failed," said Mariposa sadly, "and now I have to go home and admit it to all the people who believed in me."

The Butterfly Fairy glanced over her shoulder one last time.

"What is that?" she wondered, spotting a shadowy figure heading towards the palace.

Mariposa's heart thumped. What if this stranger was the Gwyllion? She had to warn the Crystal Fairies!

Part 2 Barbie
Mariposa
& the
Fairy Princess

Mariposa turned back to the palace. Ahead of her, she could see the figure moving amongst Shimmervale's Crystallites. One-by-one, the lights of the city began to fade.

Soon even the royal ballroom was plunged into darkness. When the glow in Catania's Crystallite necklace went out too, the Princess rushed up to the chamber at the top of the palace.

"Catania!" called Mariposa. "It's the Gwyllion! She's putting out the Crystallites!"

"If she turns all of the Crystallites into rock," warned Catania, "Shimmervale will freeze!"

The Gwyllion cackled at King Regellius as she made her way towards the Heartstone Tower.

"The Heartstone is like a candle," whispered Catania. "If we keep it lit, we can relight all the other Crystallites."

"But she's going to get there first!" gasped Mariposa.

"Shimmervale!" screeched the Gwyllion. "For your selfishness, I leave you nothing!"

"Stop!" cried Mariposa.

The brave Butterfly Fairy darted towards the Heartstone, but the Gwyllion was too quick. She blasted Mariposa with her staff, freezing her to the spot.

The Heartstone began to crumble. Mariposa was helpless to stop the destruction, but her new friend wasn't. Somehow the Princess found the courage to overcome her fear of flying.

"You won't stop me this time, little one!" hissed the Gwyllion.

The wicked fairy was wrong. Catania pulled the staff out of her hand, sending it tumbling to the ground.

Cr-ack! The magic staff broke in two.

"You made it!" cheered Mariposa.

Catania's face lit up.

The Gwyllion had been defeated, but the Heartstone still looked cold.

"Look in your pocket!" cried Mariposa.

Catania lifted out the delicate Flutter Flower her new friend had given to her.

"Hold it close to the Heartstone," suggested Mariposa.

Slowly but surely, the light inside the giant Crystallite began to grow. Suddenly a multi-coloured rush of energy flooded through it.

The fairies looked on in wonder as the power of the Heartstone and Flutter Flower transformed them, too. Mariposa and Catania's wings both began to grow.

The gift of the Flutter Flower's magic was all that the Heartstone needed. The glow in its core grew brighter and brighter.

"It's working!" marvelled Catania.

Whoosh!

A burst of colour cascaded in all directions, connecting the Heartstone to all the other Crystallites in the kingdom. The palace, city and Glow Water Falls were all brought back to life! Soon every Crystallite in the land was shining once more.

King Regellius
rushed into the chamber.
Could Catania really be flying?

"Mariposa," said the King
humbly. "I owe you an apology. I
misjudged you."

"Where's my staff?"
muttered the Gwyllion,
staggering to her feet.

King Regellius was ready to wreak his revenge,
but Catania stopped him.

"Remember why all this happened," she urged. "The
Gwyllion only asked us for one Crystallite."

The Princess gently put the Crystallite necklace round
the Gwyllion's neck.

"Thank you," she said. "I hope I can live up to
your faith in me."

It was time for Mariposa to return to Flutterfield, but she wasn't going alone – all of Shimmervale were coming, too! Queen Marabella hosted a grand ball to celebrate the new friendship between the kingdoms.

"It is an honour to meet your highness," said King Regellius, presenting her majesty with a carved wooden box.

Queen Marabella was thrilled to find a stunning Crystallite necklace inside!

Beautiful music began to play.

"Care to dance?' said Prince Carlos, taking Mariposa's hand.

The Butterfly Fairy smiled.

"I'd love to!"

Crystal Ball Quiz

The Crystal Ball should have been a shimmering success, but it ended in disaster! When Mariposa dropped the Crystallite necklace that the princess had given her, the King announced that she could not be trusted.

Take a look at this picture of the Shimmervale palace ballroom, then try and answer the quiz questions. Check your answers at the back of the book, then colour in a crystal for every one you get right.

1 Who is floating in the air beside Mariposa?

2 What colour is King Regellius' boots?

3 What is falling from Mariposa's neck?

4 Who is standing behind the King?

5 How many guests can you count in the background?

Mariposa
Colour-by-numbers

Mariposa truly is the smartest fairy in Flutterfield! At first King Regellius said the Butterfly Fairy's wings were strange and ungainly, but soon he came to see how beautiful the royal ambassador really was.

Look at this magical portrait of Mariposa. Now use the number to key to bring the picture to life in all the right colours!

1

2

3

4

5

6

I Can Be ... You Can Be...

Did you know that you can be anything that you want to be?
All it takes is hard work, dedication and a bright imagination! Finding the right challenge takes time and thought. You need to find something that suits you in every way.

Read the personality descriptions, then draw a line to match them up to the job that would suit them best. Which of these girls sounds like you?

There are no right or wrong answers, the choices are up to you!

The best person for this job has a real connection with animals - large or small. They are happiest outdoors or walking in the park.

This is a job for a natural adventurer! This person loves going on holidays to unusual places and exploring the world around them. They are quick to learn new things.

This career would suit an arty type who has a practical side, too. This person's work is neat and precise, but they also have a big imagination.

The ideal candidate for this role is a fashionista who loves sketching and making things. To do the job they need statement style and an eye for colour.

This is the perfect job for a curious person who likes to keep up with all the latest news! A natural communicator, they are bright, chatty and quick-thinking.

The person who does this job best is crazy about technology. They are totally into cool gadgets and apps! If something gets broken, they are the one who can fix it.

Fashion Designer

Architect

TV Presenter

Pilot

Vet

Computer Technician

What job would suit you best? Draw yourself in your dream role here! Underneath describe the sort of things you would need to do and clothes you would wear.

One day, ... could be a ....

....

....

....

BOY STORY

Ken, Steven and Ryan are the guys that we hang out with - they're so cool! The boys are always there to share a joke or tell us about the latest happening party. Ken has lived next door to me since forever, and I've known Steven ages, too. I first saw Ryan playing guitar at a gig in town. His music was so awesome, I ran up to introduce myself!

Ken is laid-back and relaxed, just like his style!

The Essential Ken

Ken and I grew up together, so our friendship is very special. Sometimes we even finish each other's sentences! As well as being the school soccer star and all round sports champ, Ken is sensitive, fun, loyal and true.

Eyes:
Blue

Hair:
Blonde

Height:
188cm

Pets:
Hudson

The Essential Steven

I only have to look at Steven and I giggle – he's a funny guy! He's definitely the person to call if you want to get the party started. Steven is a smart, too. He's a genius with computers and gadgets.

Ryan is a natural born rock star. Check out the leather jacket and shades!

The Essential Steven

Raquelle's twin Ryan is the quiet, brooding type. That's because he's crazy about music! He's always tapping out tunes and scribbling down lyrics. Ryan may look tough, but he's got a heart of gold.

Steven is a big fan of graphic tees. He never goes anywhere without his MP3!

Eyes: Brown

Hair: Dark brown

Height: 190cm

Pets: Ruff

Eyes: Brown

Hair: Dark brown

Height: 183cm

Pets: None

That's the rest of the gang! Aren't they great? There is just one more very special group that you really ought to meet. Flip forward to page 72.

Thrill Seekers

Have you ever been skiing? It takes a while to learn, but there's nothing like whooshing down a mountain with the wind in your hair! This photo was taken on my last winter holiday. I thought I was on my own, but one of my cheeky pets snuck into my suitcase and joined in the fun!

Can you spot the secret stowaway?

Write the pet's name here, then draw a picture of them in their snow gear.

_ _ _ _ _ _

Mystery Visitor

I've got someone special coming over this evening. I can't wait to see them! We're going to have supper, play music and gossip all night.

Any ideas who the mystery visitor might be? Use the clues at the bottom of the page to help you cross names off of the grid. The last person left will be your answer!

Clues:

1. The visitor is female.

2. We are not related.

3. They have dark hair.

4. Their eyes are brown.

Ken

Raquelle

Summer

Skipper

Ryan

Nikki

Steven

Teresa

Stacie

The mystery visitor is...

....

Pet Perfection

I'm absolutely animal mad! Are you? My pets are part of my family. It takes lots of time to look after them all properly, but it's worth every second. Tawny and co give me heaps of love in return! A ride round the paddock, a walk with the pups or a purrtastic cuddle with Blissa are all I need to start my day with a smile.

Tawny is my beloved horse. She has a coat like caramel and a tumbling golden mane. I learnt to ride on Tawny – she taught me how to trot, canter and jump. On the weekends I love going to the stables to visit her new baby colt.

Last year was the best birthday ever – all my friends surprised me with a Chihuahua puppy! Lacey is utterly adorable and a bit cheeky, too. When the girls come over the gets so excited she runs around in circles!

My Special Pet

Have you a pet that's special to you? Perhaps you dream of owning one some day? Write about them below.

Name: ....

Animal: ....

Why I love them: ....
....
....

Draw a pet portrait here.

Taffy is the most loyal and gentle friend any girl could wish for! She and I have grown up together. When I first got her all those years ago, I never thought I'd see the day when Taffy had puppies of her own.

Sequin is my diamond in the ruff! I was jogging in the park one day when I spotted a lost, dirty puppy. I cleaned her up and discovered a stunning show poodle! Nobody stepped forward to claim Sequin, but I was thrilled to give her a home.

I share Blissa with my sisters – she's our cute little princess! kitty loves dressing up in sparkly tiaras and dinky accessories. Her favourite time of day is the evening when I sit down to groom her snowy white fur.

Stars in the Shadows

The girls are ready to party, but the lights have gone out! It's tricky to work out who is who in the dark. Take a peek at the shadows, then draw a line to connect each one to the person that they belong to.

Dress Designer

I've been invited to a movie premiere tonight - what a treat! The whole city will be coming out to line the red carpet, so I'll need to look my absolute best.

Would you design a glamorous gown for me to wear?

Pick your favourite pencils or crayons, then imagine my dream dress. What shape will it be? What fabric will you choose? Will it be shiny and sparkly, or sleek and simple? The choice is up to you!

Ingredients for a FAB WINTER

I've got a good feeling about this winter. It's going to be our best yet! I've been thinking of the things that make these frosty months fun and fabulous. Can you add to the list?

- Glam winter boots
- Wrapping presents
- Cosy afternoons by the fire
- Snowball fights
- Glitzy Christmas parties
- Hot chocolate and marshmallows
- Special times with friends
- Decorating the tree
- Bundling up in winter woolies
- Playing with my pets
- Frost twinkling in the trees
- ....
- ....
- ....
- ....

Love and hugs for a fab winter!

Barbie xxx

Answers

Page 8
Mixed Up Mall
1. DRESS
2. NAIL POLISH
3. HANDBAG
4. LIPGLOSS
5. BOOTS

Page 11.
Shh... Surprise!
Chelsea = Teddy Bear
Ryan = Book
Teresa = Gloves
Raquelle = Mirror
Skipper = Headphones
Stacie = trainers

Page 28
Scholastic Fantastic

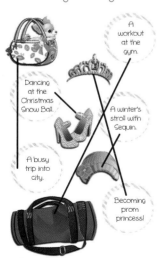

Page 29
Bags & Bling

A workout at the gym.

Dancing at the Christmas Snow Ball.

A winter's stroll with Sequin.

A busy trip into city.

Becoming prom princess!

Page 31
Ready to Party!
1. Raquelle's corsage is missing.
2. Teresa's hairband has changed colour.
3. A flower from Barbie's dress is missing.
4. Nikki's necklace is missing.
5. A handbag is missing from the background.

Page 32
It's a Barbie World!
1. Taffy
2. Chelsea
3. Lacey
4. Steven
5. Ice Skating
6. Raquelle
7. Pink
8. b
9. Skipper
10. Racetrack

Page 46
Livin' The Dream
I'm going to the MOVIES!

Page 47
Sequin Search - C

Page 50

Page 52.
Get Connected
Trail 'a' will lead Skipper to the disco

Page 54
Christmas Crossword

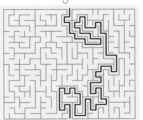

Page 64
Crystal Ball Quiz
1. Zee
2. Black
3. The Crystallite necklace
4. Princess Catania
5. 5

Page 70
Thrill Seekers
Lacey is the secret stowaway.

Page 71
The Mystery Visitor is Nikki.

Page 74
Stars in the Shadows

Barbie Annual 2014

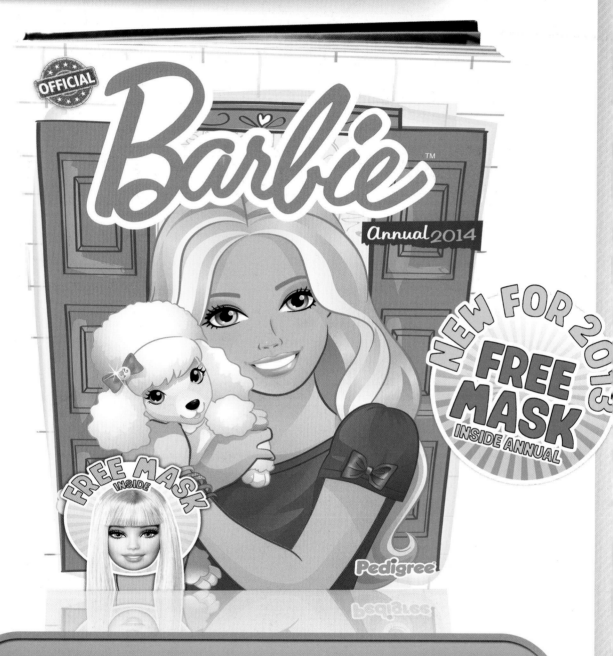

Visit www.pedigreebooks.com

Pedigree Books, Beech Hill House, Walnut Gardens, Exeter EX4 4DH